To: _____Dave_____

From: _____Mom_____

Love you lots, Dave!

the**Coupon**Collection™

SOURCEBOOKS, INC.®
NAPERVILLE, ILLINOIS

dear
grad

{ a coupon gift of congratulations }

SOURCEBOOKS, INC.
NAPERVILLE, ILLINOIS

Published by Sourcebooks, Inc.
P.O. Box 4410, Naperville, Illinois 60567-4410
(630) 961-3900
FAX: (630) 961-2168
www.sourcebooks.com

ISBN 1-4022-0069-2
Printed and bound in the United States of America
DR 10 9 8 7 6 5 4 3 2

Dear Grad, because you are special to me, I will stock the refrigerator with your favorite foods.

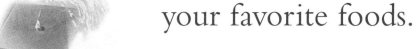

the**Coupon**Collection™

SOURCEBOOKS, INC.®
NAPERVILLE, ILLINOIS

Dear Grad, I will help you rearrange your room or move when you leave home.

the**Coupon**Collection™

SOURCEBOOKS, INC.®
NAPERVILLE, ILLINOIS

This coupon entitles the grad to a frame for that **great picture** of you receiving your diploma!

theCouponCollection™

SOURCEBOOKS, INC.®
NAPERVILLE, ILLINOIS

Off the Hook Coupon.
The grad does not have to answer any more questions on your future plans!

theCouponCollection™

SOURCEBOOKS, INC.™
NAPERVILLE, ILLINOIS

Keep in Touch Coupon.

This entitles the grad to

a box of stationery so

you can write to

those you love.

theCouponCollection™

SOURCEBOOKS, INC.®
NAPERVILLE, ILLINOIS

Calming Coupon.

Treat yourself to a cup
of cocoa and stop
worrying about what
the future holds!

the**Coupon**Collection™

SOURCEBOOKS, INC.®
NAPERVILLE, ILLINOIS

Dear Grad, this coupon entitles you to a celebratory meal at the restaurant of your choice!

the**Coupon**Collection™

SOURCEBOOKS, INC.®
NAPERVILLE, ILLINOIS

Just Like the Movies Coupon

Let's go to the movie store and rent movies about recent graduates!

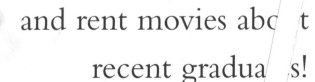

the**Coupon**Collection™

SOURCEBOOKS, INC.®
NAPERVILLE, ILLINOIS

Picture This Coupon.

Grad, I'll help you make a
scrapbook of your
school memories.

theCouponCollection™

SOURCEBOOKS, INC.®
NAPERVILLE, ILLINOIS

Dear Grad, because you're just getting started on your own, let me pay the next time we go for coffee or ice cream.

theCouponCollection™

SOURCEBOOKS, INC.
NAPERVILLE, ILLINOIS

Dear Grad, let me be the first to refer to you as an alum of your school!

the**Coupon**Collection™

SOURCEBOOKS, INC.®
NAPERVILLE, ILLINOIS

Dear Grad, let me tell you how proud I am of you by writing you a letter listing all of the reasons you're special to me.

theCouponCollection™

SOURCEBOOKS, INC.®
NAPERVILLE, ILLINOIS

This coupon entitles the grad to one free phone card so you can keep in touch from anywhere!

theCouponCollection™

SOURCEBOOKS, INC.®
NAPERVILLE, ILLINOIS

This coupon entitles the grad to an address book to keep track of friends and loved ones.

theCouponCollection™

SOURCEBOOKS, INC.®
NAPERVILLE, ILLINOIS

Hit the Road Coupon:

Good for one weekend road trip (gas included!)

the**Coupon**Collection™

SOURCEBOOKS, INC.®
NAPERVILLE, ILLINOIS

Dear Grad, I'll pay for your ticket to your first Homecoming game.

theCouponCollection™

SOURCEBOOKS, INC.®
NAPERVILLE, ILLINOIS

New You Coupon.

Let's go shopping and
pick out an outfit for

the first day of your
new adventure!

the**Coupon**Collection™

SOURCEBOOKS, INC.
NAPERVILLE, ILLINOIS

This coupon entitles the grad to one roll of **quarters** to use in the laundromat.

the**Coupon**Collection™

SOURCEBOOKS, INC.®
NAPERVILLE, ILLINOIS

This coupon entitles the grad  to cooking lessons so you can prepare scrumptious meals for yourself.

the**Coupon**Collection™

SOURCEBOOKS, INC.®
NAPERVILLE, ILLINOIS

Weekend Retreat Coupon.

Come back home
(or stay home) and
be pampered by
your family!

the**Coupon**Collection™

SOURCEBOOKS, INC.®
NAPERVILLE, ILLINOIS

Guest Chef Coupon.

I will prepare a

meal for you!

theCouponCollection™

SOURCEBOOKS, INC.®
NAPERVILLE, ILLINOIS

Dear Grad, let me help you pick out your first suit.

theCouponCollection™

SOURCEBOOKS, INC.
NAPERVILLE, ILLINOIS

Pack It Up Coupon.

Grad, I will help you
decide what to keep
and what to get rid of.

the**Coupon**Collection™

SOURCEBOOKS, INC.®
NAPERVILLE, ILLINOIS

Small World Coupon.

Grad, I will introduce you
to people I know who
can further your
ambitions.

theCouponCollection™

SOURCEBOOKS, INC.®
NAPERVILLE, ILLINOIS

Dear Grad, you can
use me as a reference
anytime!

the**Coupon**Collection™

SOURCEBOOKS, INC.®
NAPERVILLE, ILLINOIS

This coupon is good
for one late-night
phone call
when you're
feeling blue.

theCouponCollection™

SOURCEBOOKS, INC.®
NAPERVILLE, ILLINOIS

This coupon entitles the grad to one colorful pet fish to keep you company.

theCouponCollection™

SOURCEBOOKS, INC.®
NAPERVILLE, ILLINOIS

Dear Grad, I will send you cards periodically to let you know I'm thinking of you.

theCouponCollection™

SOURCEBOOKS, INC.®
NAPERVILLE, ILLINOIS

Dear Grad, tell me your favorite story from your school years.

theCouponCollection™

SOURCEBOOKS, INC.®
NAPERVILLE, ILLINOIS

Dear Grad, let's share our dreams for the future with each other.

theCouponCollection™

SOURCEBOOKS, INC.
NAPERVILLE, ILLINOIS

Art Attack Coupon.

This coupon entitles

the grad to a poster to

spiff up your room!

the**Coupon**Collection™

SOURCEBOOKS, INC.®
NAPERVILLE, ILLINOIS

Still Caring Coupon.

Even though you're on your
own now, I will send you a care
package to let you know
I'm thinking of you.

theCouponCollection™

SOURCEBOOKS, INC.®
NAPERVILLE, ILLINOIS

Dear Grad,

I will come visit you

on your birthday—

and bring a present!

The Coupon Collection

Sourcebooks, Inc.®
Naperville, Illinois

Pig Out Coupon.

Grad, you've worked so hard—

now let's celebrate with

all our favorite desserts!

the**Coupon**Collection™

SOURCEBOOKS, INC.®
NAPERVILLE, ILLINOIS

Dear Grad, take me to your favorite place.

theCouponCollection™

SOURCEBOOKS, INC.®
NAPERVILLE, ILLINOIS

Dear Grad, let's look at pictures from *all* of your school years—from kindergarten to now—and see how much you've changed.

the**Coupon**Collection™

SOURCEBOOKS, INC.®
NAPERVILLE, ILLINOIS

Dear Grad, tell me the most valuable thing you learned in school.

theCouponCollection™

SOURCEBOOKS, INC.®
NAPERVILLE, ILLINOIS

Dear Grad, I will help you address thank-you notes for all of the graduation presents you received.

theCouponCollection™

SOURCEBOOKS, INC.®
NAPERVILLE, ILLINOIS

This coupon entitles the grad to one night of **reminiscing** with friends about how much fun your school years were.

theCouponCollection™

SOURCEBOOKS, INC.®
NAPERVILLE, ILLINOIS

❧ from **me** to **you** ❧

Dear Grad: A Coupon Gift of Congratulations

I Love You Dad: A Coupon Gift of Love and Thanks

I Love You Mom: A Coupon Gift of Love and Thanks

Best of Friends: A Coupon Gift of Love and Thanks

Available at your local gift store or bookstore or by calling (800) 727-8866.

Collect them all!

✑ a breath of fresh air ✑

Going Over the Hill Slowly: A Coupon Gift That Keeps You Young
The Wild Side of Womanhood: A Coupon Gift to Unleash Your Audacious Power
Get a Grip: A Coupon Gift to Put You Back in Charge
The Goddess Within: A Coupon Gift that Celebrates You

✑ the country life ✑

I Love You Grandma: A Unique Tear-Out Coupon Gift of Love and Thanks
Dear Mom: A Unique Tear-Out Coupon Gift Just for You
Country Cat: A Unique Tear-Out Coupon Gift for the Feline Lover
A Country Life Wherever You Are: A Unique Tear-Out Coupon Gift for a Simpler Life

Available at your local gift store or bookstore or by calling (800) 727-8866.

Collect them all!

❧ a gift for the spirit ❧

Simple Serenity: A Coupon Gift to Help and Support You
A Little Bit of Feng Shui: A Coupon Gift to Gently Shift Your Energies
A Little Bit of Yoga: A Coupon Gift to Energize and Relax You
Living in Abundance: A Coupon Gift to Enhance and Enrich You

❧ a drop of sunshine ❧

Slow Down: A Book of Peaceful Coupons
Faith, Hope and Love: A Coupon Gift to Restore Your Spirit
Angels: A Coupon Gift of Miracles
The Artist in You: A Coupon Gift to Spark Your Creativity

Available at your local gift store or bookstore or by calling (800) 727-8866.

Collect them all!

theCoupon Collection™

SOURCEBOOKS, INC.®
NAPERVILLE, ILLINOIS